REDJADEMARTIALARTS.COM

Copyright © 2017 by Neil Ripski

www.redjademartialarts.com

All rights reserved. This book or any portion thereof may not be reproduced or used in any manner whatsoever without the express written permission of the publisher except for the use of brief quotations in a book review.

Printed in partnership with Lulu.com Self Publishing.

First Printing, 2017

ISBN 978-0-9939634-3-8

Edited, compiled, and designed by One Cent Press

One Cent Press
6352 184 ST NW
Edmonton, AB, T5T2N8
www.onecentpress.com

1 3 5 7 9 8 6 4 2

Gu Yu Cheung's Iron Palm Method

Internal Qigong Training

NOTE

The most important part of this or any qigong practice is to avoid qigong bing 氣功病 (qigong sickness) which is most often related to creation of heat through visualization and imagination.

Heavy hands has a mantra that one must keep in mind in order not only to gain the full benefit of the training but also to avoid qigong sickness...

"the bones are light and cool, /
the flesh is heavy and wet."

Be sure the body cools after the postures are finished!
Do not seek to continue with the feeling of warmth.
Do not chase the fire.

Heavy Hands Iron Palm / Iron Body Qigong
重手鐵體氣功

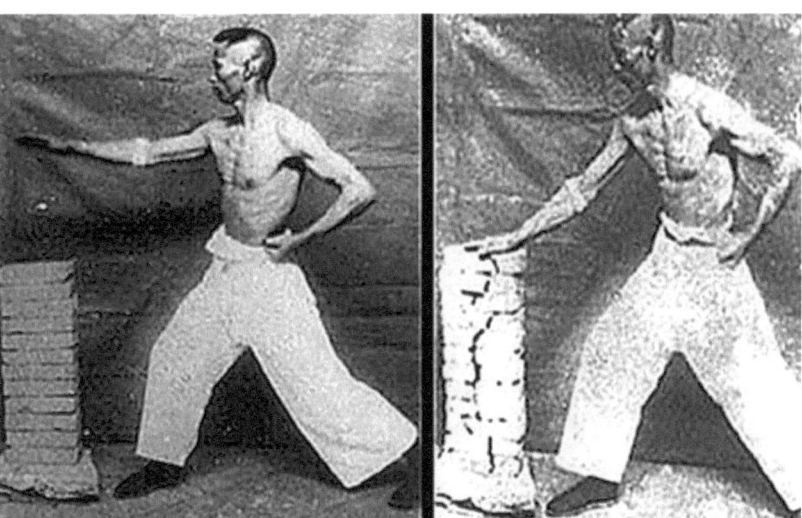

Gu Yu Cheung's Heavy Hands is possibly one of the best kept secret Iron Palm methods in Chinese Martial Arts. Master Gu was an incredibly famous Northern Shaolin Master who travelled to the South to teach, answering many challenges and never losing. He is documented in the most famous iron palm photograph today – Sifu Gu himself slapping through thirteen bricks without spacers, resting on the earth. There is even a documented account of him killing a horse with a single palm strike on the neck as it charged. Gu Yu Cheung was and is the most famous exponent of Iron Palm method during his lifetime; and his methods for some reason are still mainly kept from the public or largely unknown.

I was lucky enough to learn this qigong from my gong fu brother Professor Kevin Wallbridge, whose Sifu was a student of Northern Shaolin under one of Master Gu Yu Cheung's disciples.

Of all the iron palm / iron fist methods I have studied and trained, this system has given me the most remarkable results, it is also a safe qigong to train anytime of the year (but best if done in the fall), and it can be done daily without end.

The system is made up of three parts:

- The heavy hands qigong,
- the light air exercises, and
- the five elements strikes on the iron palm bag.

by Neil Ripski

百日筑基

Heavy Hands Qigong

重手氣功

Each posture in the qigong should be held for 8-12 breaths which should be long, slow and deep and ideally done with either Buddhist (Dantien) breathing or Daoist (Reverse) breathing.

I find that Daoist breathing brings about a more profound change during this qigong practice and if you are knowledgeable in its use, I recommend it.

The 12 postures are as follows –

Daoist Awaits the Dawn

Immortal Points the Way

Heavy Hands

Penetrate the Mountain Passes

Cradle the Celestial Embryo

Open the Window to look at the Moon

Great Solar Stance

Fire Palms

Bear down like Tai Shan

Pillar of Heaven

Spiritual Tortoise

Daoist Awaits the Dawn

Daoist Awaits the Dawn

Standing with the feet shoulder width apart and the body aligned vertically by tucking the tailbone slightly and opening the neck as though listening backwards, allow the hands to rest in their most natural state with the fingers falling as they may. Imagine a small ball under each armpit keeping this area open and free.

This qigong method focuses on releasing tension from the body because we tend to hold ourselves back when striking by tightening muscle groups that are actually an antithesis to our movement. So, release becomes very important for the delivery of power and to do this we must release all tension. In this opening posture, find the tension in your body from top to bottom as you prepare for the rest of the qigong.

8 to 12 breaths.

Immortal Points the Way

Raise the arms up to shoulder height and hold your wrists slightly higher than elbows and level with your shoulders. The arms should not be held at your sides, but should be slightly forward with the hands in your peripheral vision while you look ahead.

The hands are positioned as though the thumb and small finger were resting flat on a table top with the index finger highest and pointing outwards and the fingers turned upwards slightly.

Many of the positions have a "line of intent" within them – a place you should hold your mind while you are releasing and maintaining the position. This is the area you are training for striking. Immortal points the way has a line of intent from the index finger up the inside of the forearm to the elbow that you should place your mind on, like a clothesline with the inner arm or a filing strike.

8 to 12 breaths.

Heavy Hands

Return to the original position – Daoist awaits the Dawn and hold it the same way as before. What changes here is the experience and mental intent behind the position.

Feel the blood and lymph rushing back into the hands, filling them and making them feel heavier. Simply experience and observe the sensation of returning to this position.

8 to 12 breaths.

Penetrate the Mountain Passes

Settle the body slightly backwards as you raise the arms up until the elbows reach your ribs. Open the inside of the forearms to the sky, meaning creating a positive spiral force – Shun – that wraps outwards over your arms, and then rotate the wrists inwards to bring palms down to face the earth and creating a negative or counter flowing spiral force – Ni.

Reach the fingertips forward with the palm rounded.

The mind intent in this position flows through the fingertips growing forward across the room to touch the opposite wall, and equally the spinal processes pulling backwards in a vertical line to equalize the forward intent and force. This will allow the body to settle downwards and backwards slightly to counter-balance the forward force.

Mountain Passes trains the ability to dot (Dian 點) with the fingertips into an opponent's body.

8 to 12 breaths.

Cradle the Celestial Embryo

Bring the arms back down the front of the body and round them as though you are holding a large pregnant belly. Palms towards the underside of the belly and a small ball under each armpit. Settle deeply into the body and release as much tension as you possibly can.

The mind intent here supposes there are people pressing inwards on your rounded arms trying to crush your belly and you are holding them off with outward pressure by keeping the roundness open and filled with potential but not physical strength.

The main line of intent is from the middle finger on the outside of the forearms to the elbow. This trains back handed forearm strikes found in many martial systems.

8 to 12 breaths.

Open the Window to Look at the Moon

Sit down two inches, or five centimeters, keeping the spine straight and maintaining verticality while releasing as much tension as possible throughout your body. Bring the hands up above and in front of the head as though holding something above you with the knife edges of your hands.

The eyes should look up and forward between the fingers of the raised hands without changing the heads verticality. Look up only with your eyes and do not change the neck. Settle the tailbone downwards while pressing gently upwards with the hands creating a traction in the spine.

The line of intent in Open the Window to look at the Moon is from the end of the pinky finger through to the wrist, the knife edge of the hand. The saying is "Hand like a knife."

8 to 12 breaths.

Great Solar Stance

Bring the hands down in front of the body as though you were holding a beach ball on your chest with the palms facing the body. This is like the standard Zhang Zhuang or standing post posture but with a different mindset involved – instead of working for only relaxation (which is also a part of the great solar stance) the mindset here is explained by the poetry of the posture.

"Imagine you are holding the sun on your chest, it is expanding in all directions and you are holding it inwards and keeping it on your chest," as well as the saying "melt the snow all around you from the heat of your body".

Of course, this needs to be mentioned that heat is dangerous and so it is alright to feel the warmth of this posture (and the next) but always remember the saying for the heavy hands qigong "The bones are light and cool and the flesh is heavy and wet."

This posture trains strikes that come back towards the body with the palms of the hands.

8 to 12 breaths.

Fire Palms

Settle into the legs even more by dropping your stance straight down another four inches while bringing your arms down from the great solar stance. Place the elbows on the ribs and pull back the fingers while the heels of the palms are pressed forward and the palms opened.

The mind here follows the instruction "The fire in your legs fans the flames in your palms."

Press the feet downwards into the earth and allow the upward pressure to line directly from the feet to the palms so pressing downwards presses the palms forward. The legs should burn from the depth of the stance during this posture, training forward palm heel strikes.

Remember: "The bones are light and cool and the flesh is heavy and wet."

8 to 12 breaths.

Bear Down like Tai Shan

Stand up to the natural stance from the beginning of the set and bring the arms up the centre of the body. Your hands will pass over your heart as you reach the top of the new stance. Bring the arms from above your head, and then down and out to the sides of your shoulders, keeping them in sight of your peripheral vision.

Be sure the arms stay at the level of the shoulders with the elbows pointing downwards and the wrists and hands slightly higher than the shoulders.

Bear down like Tai Shan trains the "Arm like a sword" strikes and the mindset in this posture is that your arms are on a table top and you are allowing your heavy arms to work to drop through the table top they are resting on.

The line of intent is therefore from the tip of the pinky finger to the elbow. The hands should be held naturally but in a "knife hand" shape (Pi Zhang – Splitting palm) as though you were executing the strike.

8 to 12 breaths.

Pillar of Heaven

Bring the hands back up over the head like the posture "Open the Window to look at the Moon" but instead of the hands held like a knife, open the palms and press them upwards towards heaven. The eyes remain looking forward as well in this posture "gazing on distant mountains".

This posture is the first of the two internal Iron Body methods in the Heavy Hands qigong, the mindset here is preparing yourself to be struck from the front with a board or staff. This means you are not actually tightening the front of the "iron vest" but are ready to.

Ideally this is an act of innervation, using the mind to activate the nervous system and bringing the body just to the point of flexing the torso to protect itself, but holding back from doing the act.

If done with a great deal of mind intent the feeling in the torso sometimes resembles tingling, electricity or heat. This is what is known as the "qi feeling" traditionally and as qi is best defined as a relationship it is the feeling of a strong relationship between the mind and body (Shen and Jing 神精).

8 to 12 breaths.

Spiritual Tortoise

The fingers turn upwards and the hands are brought down the centre of the body to just below the solar plexus.

Keep the fingers pointing upwards and the palms facing one another, round the back slightly as though you were about to be struck from behind by an opponent by a board or stick.

This is the same as the Pillar of Heaven posture where you innervate the flexation of the back of the Iron Vest.

8 to 12 breaths.

Daoist Awaits the Dawn

Return to the first posture of the set and simply allow your hands to fall into their natural relationship to your elbow. Allow your body to sort out what it is feeling and naturalize to what the qigong has done, simply feel what you feel and if it is nothing that's alright too.

Spend the 8-12 breaths relaxing and experiencing the end of the qigong.

Two Jokes are present in the set and are worth mentioning. The first is the name of the posture "Immortal points the way" as since the posture is pointing in two directions it is referencing the tendency of Taoist immortals to always give confusing answers. It can also be interpreted as instruction to follow the training and experience the results for yourself rather than simply take someone else's advice or word on the results of the practice.

The second joke lies in the two names of the iron body postures at the end of the set "Pillar of Heaven" and "Spiritual Tortoise". Both names are referring to the Chinese creation myth of the huge tortoise with the world on its back and supporting the heavens on a pillar. The tortoise not only represents longevity but its shell a metaphor for the amour the practice creates. Essentially, both postures have the same name referring to the same thing.

Light Air Exercises

These exercises are another of the rarely shared aspects of this system and are very important in the integration of the whole method to achieve Iron Palm.

They should be done directly after finishing the qigong so the feeling of the heaviness is present in the hands and arms during the exercises, giving the practitioner the sensory experience of moving martially with the heavy feeling.

Each exercise should be done at least 36 times but ideally more, and be sure to train each side equally.

Thigh Strikes

Standing in Ma Bu (Horse stance) bring both palms downwards as though slapping them on a table and allow the forearms to strike the thighs on each strike.

Turn the hands over and again bring them down as though striking with the back of the hands. These are done quickly but relaxed and with a lot of heaviness.

Striking the thighs with the forearms is key so that the hands remain loose and relaxed.

Backhand

Standing in Gong Bu (Bow and Arrow Stance) the hands will rotate for these strikes in the air. The lead hand starts with back of the hand strikes at head height and the rear hand will rotate and palm strike downwards towards the floor.

Repeat 36x on both sides.

Allow the lead hand to remain loose and relaxed throughout the exercise.

Knife's Edge

Standing in Gong Bu (Bow and Arrow Stance) the next strike is knife edge of the hand forwards at head height and the rear hand continues to rotate and palm strike towards the floor.

Allow the lead hand to remain loose and relaxed throughout the exercise.

Backfist

Standing in Gong Bu (Bow and Arrow Stance) the last strike is back-fists with the lead hand while the rear hand rotates and palm strikes towards the floor.

Allow the lead hand to remain loose and relaxed throughout the exercise.

Five Elements Iron Palm Bag Work

五行铁沙掌

This is the most common type of Iron Palm training and is more widely seen.

The five elements refer to the type of power (jin 勁) that you are working to emulates with each strike, and the method of dropping the hand must be followed to gain the benefit of the bag work.

With all five strikes in a row I tend to change from hand to hand after a predetermined number of reps just to keep things even and equal in the training.

The Five Elements and their respective jins and effects on the bag are as follows.

Progress slowly and with care to avoid later in life arthritis...

Earth

土

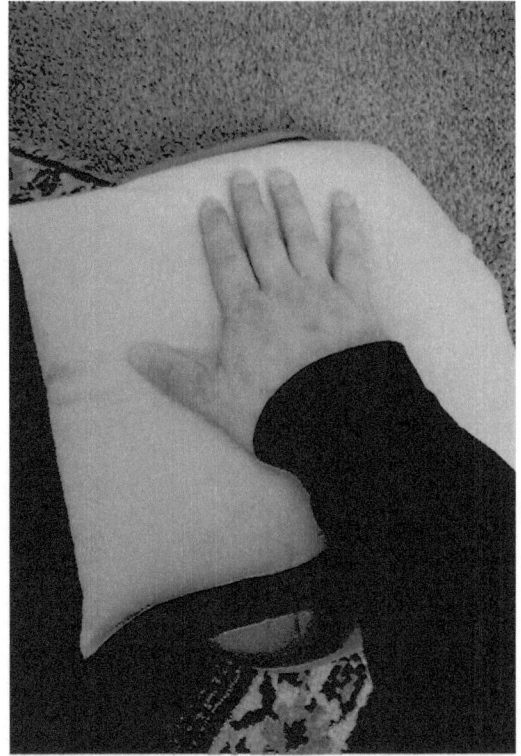

Earth 土 is the first palm strike done in the sequence and is the strike most associated with iron palm training.

Drop the centre of the palm flat onto the bag with a soft even power.

The Jin of Earth is even and should descend through the bag and stand to the floor in a horizontal, even wave. It is difficult to describe in text what a power or jin feels like but one way to look at earth jin is like a descending line of force like the = symbol. Striking from the top of the bag and descending equally through the target.

Water

水

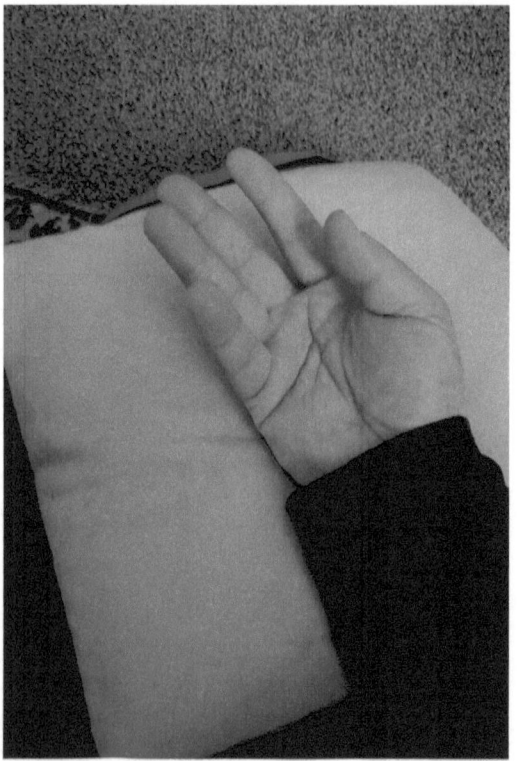

Water 水 is the second strike of the sequence and is done with the back of the hand.

After striking with the earth palm turn the hand over and drop it in a round shape on the back of the palm. Be sure to keep the fingers from striking the bag, the surface for striking is the back of the hand only.

The water palm is known by its effect on the bag. Striking in the centre of your bag the edges should 'splash' upwards as though your hand had struck water itself instead of beans. It is a round, curved power that penetrates in a smaller surface area than earth palm and has the shape like "))))) " as it drops through the bag.

Wood

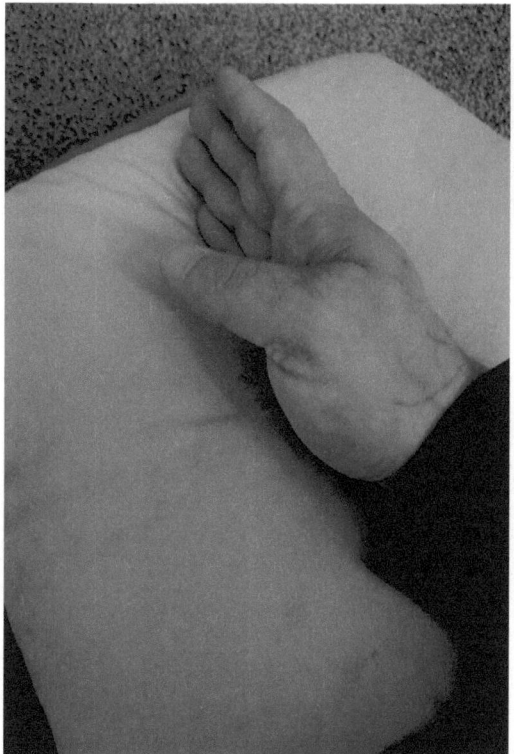

Wood 木 is the third of the strikes in the sequence and is the knife edge or chopping edge of the hand.

With the hand-held thumb up, keep the fingers together so they do not strike one another, which can result in damage to the fingers, and drop the knife edge of the hand through the bag as though you were cutting a deep trench in it.

If the bag is struck properly it will take on the shape of the trench I am mentioning when you remove your hand. Wood palm or the knife edge strike is the jin of cutting and crushing. The power cuts deeply into the bag and the stand it is on as though cleaving something in two.

Fire

火

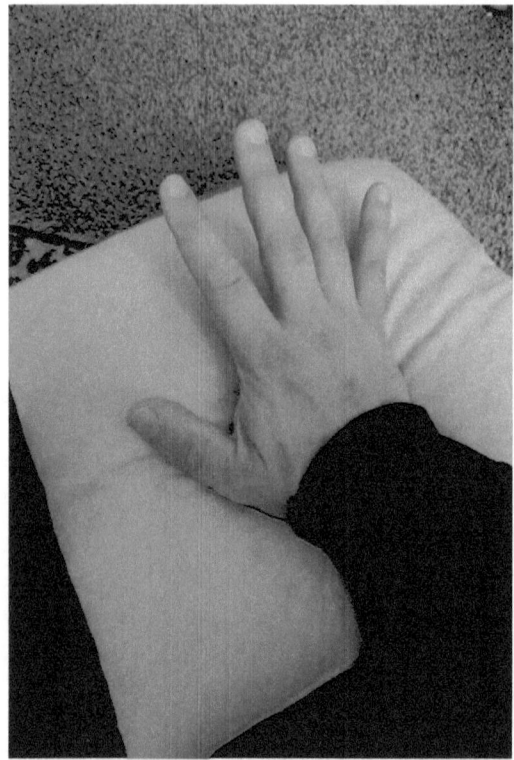

Fire 火 is the fourth strike of the sequence and has a more complex method.

While you are still dropping the hand heavily into the bag by releasing the joints, just before the moment of impact you 'pop' the palm heel and thus the ends of the radius and ulna (forearm bones) into the bag for the strike.

This method will burst the power forward through the bag from the long bones of the arm and the beans will move towards the far end of the bag each strike. The Jin of fire itself is bursting from the centre and penetrating the body of the opponent like an expanding bullet.

The heaviness of the hand coupled with the sudden burst of the hand shape at the moment of impact will create the expanding penetrating feeling in the body of the person struck.

Metal

金

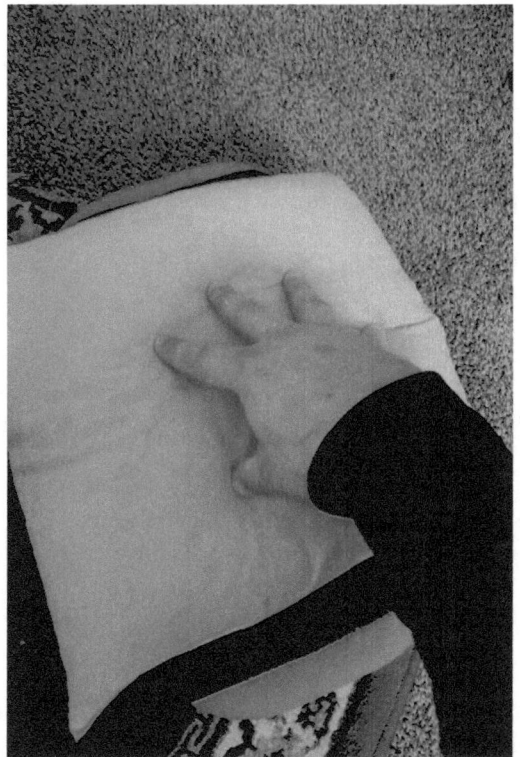

Metal 金 is the final strike and is known as 'dotting' the bag.

This is not done by all practitioners' due to the level of complexity and pain involved in making mistakes and first conditioning of the hand. This strike is to condition the fingertips and allow them to transfer spiral force through a very small surface area. Each of the five digits must hit the bag at the same time and the hand shape is crucial to avoid damaging yourself.

The hand should be held with the digits all able to strike at once and the palm cupped into a round shape to support the fingers with the bones of the hand (metacarpals).

When dropping the hand to the bag you must spiral the entire hand from the wrist inwards, so the thumb of the hand being trained is moving towards your torso as you strike. This not only creates the penetrating spiral force (the dotting jin) but as well distributes the force evenly through the digits and hand to avoid damage.

Of course, you need to be careful when training this strike and generally it will be done with less force than the others until the hand is conditioned. Avoiding injuries from training is of the utmost importance!

The Bag

鐵沙掌袋

The bag itself should be of a size bigger than your whole hand when outstretched to avoid hitting the surface underneath. In many traditions like the external Iron Palm I learned when young you change the interior of the bag over time from mung beans to sand to gravel to iron or steel shot and sometimes even progressing until you are simply slapping a rock! When I was in my early twenties I went to a stone tombstone shop and bought a piece of broken granite tombstone to use. Not the funnest thing I have ever trained.

However, in this Internal method only a bag filled with beans is used and not changed to harder materials.

This type of training is about the release of joints and as such not about the material you hit. It is not so much 'hand conditioning' but release of tension throughout the joints to allow your generated power "heaviness" to drop through your hands.

Any bag will do, filled with enough beans to avoid striking through them and hitting the surface below. Traditionally mung beans are used because they have medicinal properties for the healing of bones. However, this only works if the dust from the beans as they are crushed can get through the material of the bag and onto your hands.

If you do not have this kind of material then the type of beans becomes moot. I have mung in my bag while one of my gongfu brothers is using lentils...

...either way, if you are ever in trouble you should be able to make soup.

Releasing the Joints

This is the most important part of the bag work in the internal iron palm method and consists of three levels of training the joints to release.

Releasing the joints refers to removing all tension from the muscularity around a joint or series of joints to allow the limb to fall through the bag when training. The idea of this form of iron palm is deceptively simple, but not easy. When we extend our arm to strike someone the triceps muscle at the back of the arm fires and contracts to lengthen the arm and create force. Commonly the practitioner also clenches the bicep at the same time essentially slowing down the arm but allowing them to feel the opposing forces work on each other and feel the power they are generating – this is like driving a car with the brake pedal to the floor. It may still move forward but not at its most efficient.

When we strike we need to release the muscularity that is in opposition to the movement of the strike itself and thus stop slowing ourselves down in the transfer of force. So, to gain the iron palm aka heavy hands from this training we need to train releasing tension from the body while we strike to train our brains and nervous systems to instinctively activate in the desired way. So, we train the levels of joint release on the bag to also have the stimulus of striking an object while releasing joints.

The first level of release is at the wrist. Hovering above the bag a few inches, release the arm completely and release the wrist to drop the hand onto the bag in the various five elements shapes. While this may seem like it is not a powerful strike, it is the building of the foundation of true release throughout the body.

The second level is to release the elbow. In the same way as the wrist, hover above the bag slightly higher than before and then drop the elbow and wrist into the bag while making the shapes for the hand.

The third level is to release the shoulder, this is the more standard looking "iron palm" strike and releases directly from the shoulder through the arm. When all these joints have released and gravity is allowed to drop the hand the full force of the weight of the arm can fall into the bag. This allows for the real weight of the arm to be used as weapon or strike rather than the tension or strength of the muscles in the arm and shoulder, a much more reliable method of delivering force.

On average, a human arm weighs about ~5.3% of your total body weight, depending on your gender, among other factors. A leg is about 17.5%. This means for a 150lb average human being, an arm weighs ~8lb and a leg weighs ~26lb. When adjusted to include the hand this weight goes up to an average of 6.5% of the person's body weight. So the average 150lb person will be dropping 9lbs of body weight without any addition from the torso. A skilled internal stylist will also be able to drop Tan Zhong (centre of the chest) as a joint adding more of their torsos weight behind the strike. This is significant as the iron palm strike is more of a dropping, heavy power than a "hard" force. To add perspective the average weight of a baseball bat is approximately 2lbs and when used as a weapon has devastating or fatal effects.

Harnessing the power of relaxation and thus the weight of our own bodies creates a great deal of force over time but its training is very counter intuitive. When we think of force or power we associated it with strength and how much work we can do with our muscular strength. Allowing heavy hands to train the dropping or heavy force is a much more reliable and maintainable type of power training even into old age.

Di Da Jiu

鐵沙掌袋

The use of Dit Da Jow (Di Da Jiu 鐵沙掌袋) is mentioned elsewhere in this book including recipes so here I am only going to mention that for the training of iron palm it is important to be healing fast enough to not cause real long term damage to the hands. Use of a good herbal liniment will help to heal after each session to avoid this. If you cannot make or order either of the recipes in this book you may be able to find some commercially available ones online that will work as well.

Our friends over at plumdragonherbs.com sells Gu Yu Cheung's Iron Palm Formula pre-measured and ready to make.

Ingredients:

Safflower, Viper, Pyrite, Dragon Bone, Clematis, Acanthopanax, Frankincense, Wingless Cockroach, Sappan Wood, Cnidium, Angelica Tails, Dispacus, Catechu, Cinnamon Twig, White Peony, Bur-Reed, Auklandia, Siler, Red Peony, Tinospora, White Angelica, Notopterygium, Bugleweed, Peach Kernel, Cinnamon Bark, Akebia, Tricosanthes.

Notes:

Notes:

Notes:

Notes:

Thank you for supporting us!

Red Jade Martial Arts is dedicated to sharing knowledge of traditional Chinese Martial Arts and Medicine in an effort to promote martial virtue and wholesome well being.

Look for Sifu Ripski's other books on his Lulu.com Spotlight!

www.redjademartialarts.com

www.ingramcontent.com/pod-product-compliance
Lightning Source LLC
Chambersburg PA
CBHW022111160426
43198CB00008B/431